I0164914

# Living Without Them – My Journey With Loss
## Work Book

# By Rev. Dr. Jose H. Tate

# Contents

Living Without Them – My Journey With Loss Workbook

Copyright © 2012 Rev. Dr. José H. Tate
All rights reserved. No part of this study may be reproduced, stored in a retrieval system, or transmitted in any form, without permission of Dr. Tate.

ISBN 13: 9780988203815

All scripture quotations are taken from the New King James Version of the Holy Bible. Copyright © 1992 By Thomas Nelson, Inc.
Dr. JHT Publisher

# Outline – Seven-Week Course

Theme:  Based on "Living Without Them" Book. Overcoming life challenges, loss, and experiencing victory.

Purpose:  To experience personal and spiritual growth as we participate, share, and grow in relationship with God.

Vision:  Creating an environment that promotes appropriate processing, healing, and hope in God.

Goals for each session:

- Reflection and Contemplation
- Name and Confess
- Accept and Reject
- Plan and Commit
- Adjust and Implement
- Observe and Evaluate
- Implement and Practice

## Course Agreement:

- I agree to pray before each session

- I agree to participate and share

- I agree to respect and treat others with dignity

- I agree to disagree (if necessary), but never argue

- I agree to keep classroom disclosure confidential

- I agree to "do the work" necessary for growth

- I agree to commit myself to these sessions

Name _____ Date _____

# Material Use

The primary use for the material contained in this workbook is to be used in a small group study setting. Depending upon the number in attendance, there should be an overall facilitator and table leaders (trained to help facilitate groups prior to classes) for these sessions. There should be no less than two and no more than six per group. Facilitator will open each session with prayer, provide instructions for each session, and end each session with prayer. Since Rev. Dr. Jose H. Tate bases the workbook upon "Living Without Them – My Journey With Loss", group participants are highly encouraged to purchase this book prior to the start of these sessions. The workbook can be purchased at the beginning of class. Below is a brief description of each section within the sessions.

Scripture – The assigned scriptures are to be read and used as an introduction into each session.

Reflection – Reflection questions are designed to help participants begin to process the areas of concern.

Discovery – Used to internalize areas of concern for insights. Also, insights can be discussed with group.

Discussion – Time to listen and share with each other.

Exercise – Opportunity to share "things learned" with others.

Plan of action – Moving from process to application.

# Class 1

## The Way It Was – Growing Up

SCRIPTURE:  Genesis chapter 37:1-28 (Dysfunction)
I Kings chapter 2:1-4 (Not perfect, but...)

REFLECTION:

- Who were your family?  How did you fit in?
- What type of person was each of your family members or relatives?

DISCOVERY:

- What type of relationship did you have with each family member or relative?
- Which family member(s) or relative(s) influenced you the most?  In what way?

DISCUSSION:

- Are you carrying any hurts from those relationships? If so, what are they and how have they influenced how you think, feel, and behave?

EXERCISE:

- What things have you learned or experienced from your family that has helped you in life?

PLAN OF ACTION:

- What steps do you need to take toward healing or moving forward?

# Notes

# Class 2

## The Way It Was – Growing Up

SCRIPTURE:  Daniel chapter 1 (Challenging)
Philippians chapter 3:3-7 (Doing well)

REFLECTION:

- What type of environment did you grow up in (low income, middle income, wealthy, hostile, nurturing, supportive, etc.)?

DISCOVERY:

- Highlight things that you would consider "very good" concerning your upbringing, environment, relationships with others, personal experiences, etc.
- Highlight things that you would consider "bad" concerning your upbringing, environment, relationships with others, personal experiences, etc.
- Highlight things that you would consider "very bad" about your upbringing, environment, relationships with others, personal experiences, etc.

DISCUSSION:

- What were the most significant positive and negative experiences of your life before you turned 21 years old?

EXERCISE:

- How have these experiences influenced your life? What things do you need to accept and reject from your past?

PLAN OF ACTION:

- What steps do you need to take towards healing or moving forward?

# Notes

# Class 3

## The Way It Is – Gone But Not Forgotten

SCRIPTURE:  Genesis chapter 4:1-16  (Complex)
Genesis chapter 50:24-26 (Restored)

REFLECTION:

- Was the death of your loved one(s) unexpected or expected?

DISCOVERY:

- What was your life like a year prior to the loss of your loved one(s) – church, job, school, relationships, health, habits, etc.
- What was your loved one's life like a year prior to their death – church, job, school, relationships, health, habits, etc.

DISCUSSION:

- What was your relationship like with your loved one a year prior to their death?  Was there conflict or peace?
- Was your loved one a Christian?  How did their lifestyle and spiritual status affect you (your family) in terms of accepting their death?

EXERCISE:

- What are some positive things you can take from your departed loved one's life and God's word in dealing with the situation?

PLAN OF ACTION:

- What can help me to "let go" or wanting to control what I can't control and allow God to help me grow from the experience?

# Notes

# Class 4

## The Way It Is – Gone But Not Forgotten

SCRIPTURE:  St. John chapter 16:33 (Overcomer)
Romans chapter 8:38-39 (God's Grace)

REFLECTION:

- Were you able to connect to your loved one before he or she passed away?

DISCOVERY:

- What was your life like one year after the loss of your loved one – church, job, school, relationships, health, habits, etc.
- In what ways were you strengthened or weakened by the death of your loved one?

DISCUSSION:

- How did the death of your loved one affect others in your family?
- What helped you (and your family) cope with the death of your loved one?  Or, did the loss of this loved one cause you (and your family) to take steps backward?

EXERCISE:

- If your loved one did not live a Christian life (as far as you know), how do you still love and appreciate them?

PLAN OF ACTION:

- How do you celebrate and honor your lost loved one?  If you haven't or can't do so, why?

# Notes

# Class 5

## The Way It Can Be – Loss To Victory

SCRIPTURE:  St. John chapter 4:4 (God is greater)
Romans chapter 8:28 (God is able)

REFLECTION:

- What do you value the most in life?

DISCOVERY:

- How does your value system influence how you think, feel, and behave (make choices)?
- What is your belief system concerning God, yourself, others, the secular, life, death, sin, forgiveness, love, and hate?

DISCUSSION:

- In general, is your overall perspective positive or negative?
- What helps you understand and process loss, life challenges, and life events?
- How does your attitude affect how you respond to life?

EXERCISE:

- What helps you have a positive attitude in-spite of negativity?

PLAN OF ACTION:

- Identify areas of growth in your life and prepare a list of things that you can do on a daily/weekly basis to improve in these areas.

# Notes

# Class 6

## The Way It Can Be – Loss To Victory

SCRIPTURE:  Romans chapter 5:1-4 (Transformed)
II Corinthians chapter 1:3-4 (Empowered)

REFLECTION:

- Do you have a relationship with God?  If not, why not?  If so, what type of relationship is it?

DISCOVERY:

- As a result of dealing with pain, suffering, and loss, what have you learned about yourself and others?

DISCUSSION:

- How has dealing with suffering and loss helped you to be more empathic and identify the pain of others?
- How are you influenced by God's affirmation vs. allowing the negative aspects of life to keep you down or define your life?

EXERCISE:

- How do you practice your faith in God as opposed to living life on your own terms? Do you believe there's a difference between living according to God's will and your (self-centered) will?

PLAN OF ACTION:

- Are you pursuing God's purpose, plan, and destiny for your life? If so, what does it look like each day? If not, why not, and what steps are you willing to take to commit your life to God?

# Notes

# Class 7

## Close Out Session

SCRIPTURE:  Proverbs chapter 9:9 (Word to the wise)
Psalm chapter 1:1-3 (Be blessed)

REFLECTION:

- The most meaningful aspects of this session for me were...

DISCOVERY:

- Are my expectations concerning God, self, others, and life realistic or unrealistic?
- Am I motivated and inspired to persevere, grow, and make the necessary changes in my life?  If not, why not?

DISCUSSION:

- I'm going to take responsibility for my life (attitude, choices, goals, relationships, etc.) by doing the following...
- This is how I'm going to share my life and help others as God helps me...

EXERCISE:

- What are some tangible ways I can begin to make a positive difference in the life of others?

PLAN OF ACTION:

As a result of these sessions, I'm going to do the following:

- I'm going to seek counsel, find a mentor or responsibility partner, join a church and small group, get active in the community, devote myself to bible study, prayer, and meditation, exercise, etc.
- I'm going to do the following in evaluating and assessing my self-esteem, relationship with God and others daily...
- I'm going to find positive ways to celebrate my departed loved one(s) by doing the following...

# Notes

www.ingramcontent.com/pod-product-compliance
Lightning Source LLC
Chambersburg PA
CBHW080537030426

42337CB00023B/4774